50 Quick Ways to Help your Students Secure A and B Grades at GCSE

By Mike Gershon

Text Copyright © 2014 Mike Gershon

All Rights Reserved

About the Author

Mike Gershon is a teacher, trainer and writer. He is the author of twenty books on teaching, learning and education, including a number of bestsellers, as well as the co-author of one other. Mike's online resources have been viewed and downloaded more than 2.5 million times by teachers in over 180 countries and territories. He is a regular contributor to the Times Educational Supplement and has created a series of electronic CPD guides for TES PRO. Find out more, get in touch and download free resources at www.mikegershon.com

Training and Consultancy

Mike is an expert trainer whose sessions have received acclaim from teachers across England. Recent bookings include:

- *Improving Literacy Levels in Every Classroom*, St Leonard's Academy, Sussex

- *Growth Mindsets, Effective Marking and Feedback* Ash Manor School, Aldershot

- *Effective Differentiation,* Tri-Borough Alternative Provision (TBAP), London

Mike also works as a consultant, advising on teaching and learning and creating bespoke materials for schools. Recent work includes:

- *Developing and Facilitating Independent Learning,* Chipping Norton School, Oxfordshire

- *Differentiation In-Service Training,* Charles Darwin School, Kent

If you would like speak to Mike about the services he can offer your school, please get in touch by email: mike@mikegershon.com

Other Works from the Same Authors

Available to buy now on Amazon:

How to use Differentiation in the Classroom: The Complete Guide

How to use Assessment for Learning in the Classroom: The Complete Guide

How to use Questioning in the Classroom: The Complete Guide

How to use Discussion in the Classroom: The Complete Guide

How to Teach EAL Students in the Classroom: The Complete Guide

More Secondary Starters and Plenaries

Secondary Starters and Plenaries: History

Teach Now! History: Becoming a Great History Teacher

The Growth Mindset Pocketbook (with Professor Barry Hymer)

How to be Outstanding in the Classroom

Also available to buy now on Amazon, the entire 'Quick 50' Series:

50 Quick and Brilliant Teaching Ideas

50 Quick and Brilliant Teaching Techniques

50 Quick and Easy Lesson Activities

50 Quick Ways to Help Your Students Secure A and B Grades at GCSE

50 Quick Ways to Help Your Students Think, Learn, and Use Their Brains Brilliantly

50 Quick Ways to Motivate and Engage Your Students

50 Quick Ways to Outstanding Teaching

50 Quick Ways to Perfect Behaviour Management

50 Quick and Brilliant Teaching Games

50 Quick and Easy Ways to Outstanding Group Work

50 Quick and Easy Ways to Prepare for Ofsted

50 Quick and Easy Ways Leaders can Prepare for Ofsted

About the Series

The 'Quick 50' series was born out of a desire to provide teachers with practical, tried and tested ideas, activities, strategies and techniques which would help them to teach brilliant lessons, raise achievement and engage and inspire their students.

Every title in the series distils great teaching wisdom into fifty bite-sized chunks. These are easy to digest and easy to apply – perfect for the busy teacher who wants to develop their practice and support their students.

Acknowledgements

As ever I must thank all the fantastic colleagues and students I have worked with over the years, first while training at the Institute of Education, Central Foundation Girls' School and Nower Hill High School and subsequently while working at Pimlico Academy and King Edward VI School in Bury St Edmunds.

Thanks also to Alison and Andrew Metcalfe for a great place to write and finally to Gordon at KallKwik for help with the covers.

Table of Contents

Introduction

Model Answers

Annotated Model Answers

Marking Model Answers

Photocopy Good Work

Wall Displays

Good Work Portfolio

Justification

Teach Paragraph Structures

PEE

Writing Frames

Question Answer Frames

Structure Guidelines

Target Application

Terminology Highlighting

Terminology Quotas

Terminology Mind-Maps

Specific Success Criteria

Success Criteria Selection

Success Criteria Traffic-Lighting

Peer-Assessment

- Peer-Assessment Using Mark Schemes
- Peer-Assessment Training
- Self-Assessment Using Mark Schemes
- Self-Assessment Focussed on Targets
- Self-Assessment Checklists
- Exam Practice
- Model Answer Creation
- Bloom's Taxonomy
- Analysis
- Synthesis
- Evaluation
- A and B Grade Checklists
- Problem-Solving Techniques
- SMART Targets
- Target Tracking
- Focus on Effort and Persistence
- Build Confidence
- Problem Forecasting
- Hard Work
- Make It Fun
- Self-Reporting
- Get the Parents On-Board
- Role Models

Planned Revision

Students Teach Others

Subject Knowledge Audit

Practice, Practice, Practice

A and B Grade Revision Guides

Example Exam Scripts

Memorisation Techniques

A Brief Request

Introduction

Welcome to '50 Quick Ways to Help your Students Secure A and B Grades at GCSE.'

This book is all about the practical things we as teachers can do to help our pupils secure the very best grades in their GCSE exams and coursework.

Every entry focuses on a different idea, some of which connect together, all of which will help you to help your students achieve their potential.

As teachers we know that we can never guarantee exam grades. However, with the ideas in this book on hand, you will be in a fantastic position to help your students, giving them all the support they need to secure the A and B grades which will unlock doors for them in sixth form, work and beyond.

The techniques, strategies and activities which follow can be used across the curriculum. You can also edit and adapt them to suit your teaching style and the particular needs of your students.

So read on and enjoy.

And, of course, good luck in those exams!

Model Answers

01 If you want to help your students secure A and B grades at GCSE, where better to start than by providing them with models of what they need to do?

Models can be imitated. Models can be copied. Models can be used as the basis for our own work.

As such, models diminish the distance between where we are at and where we need to be. A young artist may begin developing their own style by using the work of a famous painter as a model. This will help them to improve the standard of their work before, over time, they develop their own style.

Using model answers in the classroom works in exactly the same way. Some exam boards provide them. Otherwise, you can make your own or photocopy student work which is of the requisite standard and use this instead.

Annotated Model Answers

02 So we have our model answers and students are using these as a guide to help them bring their own work up to the standard necessary to secure an A or a B grade. What next?

Well, why don't we provide some annotation around the outside of these model answers, indicating where marks have been picked up, where success criteria have been fulfilled and where one can find examples of excellent practice?

This development of model answers gives pupils clear, analytical guidance on what is good and why. As a result they will better understand what is expected of them and have examples on hand which they can use to help them achieve high standards.

Marking Model Answers

03 Here is a third way in which we can use model answers with our pupils.

Divide the class into pairs and give each pair a copy of the relevant GCSE mark scheme as well as a copy of a model answer.

Ask students to read through the model answer and the mark scheme, to discuss these, and then to apply the latter to the former.

Indicate that pupils should annotate the model answer, specifying where marks have been picked up, and that they should write a detailed paragraph underneath the model answer explaining what mark it should receive and why.

The whole process familiarises students with the criteria they are trying to fulfil while also giving them a model to imitate.

Photocopy Good Work

04 As you go through the year, identify student work which is particularly good; that which clearly and confidently meets the standards necessary to secure an A or B grade in your subject.

Photocopy this work, label it and begin to build up a portfolio.

By the end of the year you will have a clutch of pieces you can use in the following year to illustrate to students what it is you want them to do and different ways in which they might go about doing this.

Be sure to anonymise the work by crossing out any names or personal references.

Wall Displays

05 You can use the walls of your classroom to help pupils secure great grades at GCSE. Here are three methods you might like to employ:

- Create a display containing examples of excellent pieces of work complete with teacher feedback indicating why they are good. Encourage students to refer to this display when doing their own work.

- Create a display containing two pieces of work (one that is an A grade and one that is a B grade) with a series of annotations around them indicating what is good about the items in question. Enlarge the pieces of work and the annotations using a photocopier so that students can see them from distance.

- Create a display listing and exemplifying what is required to achieve A and B grades. Encourage pupils to use this regularly.

Good Work Portfolio

06 Create a good work portfolio to keep in your classroom for students to look through or refer to whenever they are stuck or in need of help. If you photocopy good work as suggested in entry number 4, simply place all of this in a binder and then store this prominently somewhere near the front of the class.

As an alternative, you might like to provide every pupil in your class with a portfolio of good work at the beginning of the year. They can then use this as a reference point, as a model or as a guide for their own work.

Justification

07 Across most of the curriculum higher marks are associated with the provision of justification. Anyone can assert a claim but it takes thought, knowledge and understanding to reasonably justify a claim.

As such, we can assume with a good degree of certainty that GCSE mark schemes will require justification from pupils who are seeking to achieve A and B grades. And even if they don't, being able to justify ideas and arguments indicates a sounder knowledge and understanding of the topic in question than the converse.

All of this leads us to a simple, effective piece of advice: Insist that your pupils justify any claims they make verbally or in writing. Do this continually so that they cultivate good habits, ready for their exams.

Teach Paragraph Structures

08 Paragraphs are the backbone of writing. They provide the means by which we delineate our thoughts, making it easier for the reader to understand and assimilate the information we present. As part of this process they also provide a logical sequence (or, at least, one hopes they do!) and separation of ideas.

If paragraphs are central to writing, it makes sense to teach students how to use them effectively, regardless of whether the lesson is English or not.

Paragraph structures are pre-determined ways for writing paragraphs. One of these (PEE) is explained in the next entry.

PEE

09 PEE stands for Point; Evidence; Explain. Here is an example:

This book is about helping students to secure A and B grades at GCSE (**point**). We can see this from the various entries, all of which give ideas and suggestions of how to do this (**evidence**). By presenting practical examples the book is seeking to give teachers the tools they need to help pupils to be successful (**explain**).

Teaching students to write paragraphs using this structure means giving them a tool they can always rely on; one which will help ensure they justify and develop the points they make in their writing.

You can even ask pupils to peer-assess each other's work focussing solely on the use of PEE.

Writing Frames

10 A writing frame is a means by which to structure writing. It provides students with a clear explanation of what they should write, when, and in what order. Here is an example:

1st Paragraph – Introduction

2nd Paragraph – First argument in favour

3rd Paragraph – Second argument in favour

4th Paragraph – First argument against

5th Paragraph – Second argument against

6th Paragraph – Conclusion

Giving students writing frames appropriate for A and B grade work makes it more likely they will produce text which hits the standards you want.

Over time, pupils will internalise the writing frames and should come to write in an A or B grade manner as a matter of course.

Question Answer Frames

11 As an alternative to writing frames, you can use question answer frames to help your students secure A and B grades.

Get hold of the past exam papers and mark schemes for your subject and analyse the different question types which come up. Having done this, work out various frameworks students could use to answer the different question types. Then, teach these to your pupils.

Follow up with plenty of practice during which students apply the frameworks to mock exam questions. Repetition is important if you want your pupils to internalise the frameworks and to become habituated to their use.

Structure Guidelines

12 It may be the case that your subject does not have exam questions conducive to the provision of writing frames or question answer frames (as outlined in the previous two entries). If this is the case you can provide your pupils with more general structure guidelines instead.

This involves explaining to students what they should aim to include and in roughly what order they should include this when answering certain types of question. By necessity the advice here will be vaguer but that does not mean that it loses efficacy.

On the contrary, support of this type will give students clear purchase when tackling exam questions which ask for more discursive answers than those which can be dealt with through a specific writing or answer frame.

Target Application

13 A great deal of research illustrates the link between effective feedback, rapid progress and high achievement (see, for example, Hattie 2008 and 2011; and Black et al 2003).

One of the most important elements of effective feedback is providing students with opportunities to apply the targets you have set them.

If you want to help your pupils secure A and B grades, set relevant targets and then provide time in lessons when students can apply these.

One example involves asking pupils to write their target at the top of a piece of work, to attempt to apply it during the course of their work, and then to write a paragraph at the end reflecting on whether they were successful or not.

Terminology Highlighting

14 One thing common to nearly all GCSE examinations is the awarding of marks for correct use of terminology. And we know that students who tend to be more successful in exams are the ones who have a good grasp of the language of the subject in question.

It is thus sensible for us to focus on terminology if we want to help pupils achieve the best grades.

A simple technique involves handing out a set of highlighter pens at the end of a lesson or piece of work and asking students to highlight all the terminology they have used in their writing. Having done this, invite pairs to reflect on whether or not they have done enough to be really successful.

As a follow-up, you may like to ask pupils to repeat the activity every other week for a few months. During this period, their aim will be to achieve a higher level of highlighting on each occasion.

Terminology Quotas

15 Staying on the theme of terminology, here is an alternative approach to ensuring excellent use of keywords across the board.

When you set students a piece of written work, indicate as one of the success criteria what your terminology quota is for the piece of work. That is, the minimum number of keywords every student must include in their writing.

To assist pupils, you might like to provide a pool of words from which they can select the ones they feel are most appropriate.

As an aside, it is worth noting that you can use this approach with discussion activities as well as for written work.

Terminology Mind-Maps

16 And so we come to our third terminology-inspired strategy.

Ask your students to create terminology mind-maps, either in class or at home. These should contain the topic name at the centre of the page with relevant keywords spraying out. Ideally, definitions, examples and images (to aide recall) will accompany the various keywords.

After pupils have made their mind-maps, encourage them to use these whenever they are writing about or discussing the topic in question.

If you have not come across mind-maps before, you can find out more at thinkbuzan.com.

Specific Success Criteria

17 Success criteria are those things we tell students they need to do in order to be successful in a given piece of work.

If we want to help pupils secure A and B grades at GCSE, it is as well to give them specific success criteria which closely connect to this aim whenever we ask them to complete a piece of work.

Two benefits will follow.

First, students will use their time more effectively, directing their energies towards that which is most relevant. Second, they will be more likely to develop a clear sense of precisely what it is they need to do in order to be successful in their final exams.

Success Criteria Selection

18 You can encourage self-reflection and a greater awareness of strengths and weaknesses in relation to the GCSE exams by providing students with five relevant success criteria for a piece of work and then asking them to choose the 2 or 3 they feel they would most benefit from focussing on.

The selection process will cause pupils to think carefully about what they can do and what they want to be able to do. It will also help them to develop greater metacognitive abilities (thinking about thinking).

You might like to supplement the approach by asking pupils to write a reflection at the end of their work explaining why they choose their success criteria and what resulted from this.

Success Criteria Traffic-Lighting

19 Present your students with a task and a set of success criteria which, if fulfilled, should lead to pupils securing A and B grades.

At the end of the task, ask your students to go back over their work and self-assess it using a traffic light system and the original criteria.

They should analyse how successfully they have met each success criterion before indicating after their work whether it is green (good), amber (OK) or red (in need of improvement).

Pupils can then use these findings to set themselves a target for the next lesson.

Peer-Assessment

20 Peer-assessment is a great way to open up success criteria and to expose students to different ways of approaching their work and learning.

Here are two ways in which to structure peer-assessment:

- Divide the class into pairs. Students swap work with their partner. The teacher provides a mark scheme or success criteria. Pupils use these to mark the work they have been given. They then provide feedback by way of discussion.

- Collect in student work, shuffle it and then redistribute to the class at random. Pupils use success criteria or a mark scheme to assess whoever's work they have been given. They then find the author and provide feedback orally or in writing.

Peer-Assessment Using Mark Schemes

21 We intimated in the last entry that it is useful to make mark schemes a part of peer-assessment. Taking this a step further, we can say that it is vitally important to use mark schemes in peer-assessment when we are trying to secure A and B grades at GCSE.

This is because those mark schemes (which should be from the exam board) will give students clear guidance on precisely what they need to do in order to secure high marks.

Through the process of applying the mark scheme to their peer's work, pupils will gain a great insight into what examiners will be looking for come the end of Year 11.

Peer-Assessment Training

22 In order for peer-assessment to be most effective, you need to give students a little bit of training. In short, this involves two different things:

- First, spend some time talking about the mark scheme or success criteria with your pupils. Explain to them how one goes about applying these to a piece of work.

- Second, train pupils in the language of feedback. Give them examples, models and word banks to use. Steer them away from generalities and towards specific comments connected to learning which clearly reference the mark scheme or success criteria.

Self-Assessment Using Mark Schemes

23 As with peer-assessment, so with self-assessment. Building regular mark scheme led self-assessment into your teaching will help ensure your students become closely acquainted with what examiners expect from them.

You might even like to provide pupils with a tracker sheet they can use to record the results of their own self-assessment. This will help them to analyse the way in which the quality of their work is developing and changing over time.

Self-Assessment Focussed on Targets

24 We mentioned earlier (entry 13) how important it is to give targets and then to provide opportunities for pupils to apply these targets in their work.

Developing this theme, we can see that self-assessment focussed on targets will be highly beneficial. This is for two reasons.

First, it will encourage students to actively reflect on whether or not they are implementing their targets, as well as the effects this is having on the quality of their work.

Second, it will allow pupils to set themselves new targets if they have met their present ones, or to re-focus on meeting their current ones if they have not yet succeeded in doing so.

Self-Assessment Checklists

25 Checklists are another tool through which we can help students to habituate themselves into the demands of A and B grade work.

You can create a checklist to give to your pupils containing 3-5 questions which, if answered in the affirmative, will confirm that the work in question is meeting the standards necessary for top marks.

Pupils can refer to these checklists again and again. They can even use them during the course of their work (rather than waiting until after they have finished).

Exam Practice

26 Practice makes perfect. Never a truer word was said. Proof of the fact abounds: sport; driving; cookery; writing; dancing; playing a musical instrument. And as for the myth that some people just have natural talent? Pah! It is not the case. Some people may find themselves with a better starting point but if they do not practise then it will all be for naught.

Using exam practice as part of your teaching will familiarise students with exam-style questions and the vagaries of exam technique.

If you combine exam practice with peer- or self-assessment as well as discussion and reflection, then pupils will also develop a clearer understanding of what the examiners expect of them.

Model Answer Creation

27 Here is a simple activity you can use with any class you teach. It works as follows:

Divide the class into pairs and introduce an exam question. Provide students with a mark scheme for the question, one per pair.

Set pairs the task of producing a model answer based on the question and the information provided through the mark scheme.

The nature of the question will determine the amount of time you need to give for this.

When sufficient time has passed, ask pairs to team up into fours. Groups should now discuss the different model answers they have produced. Pairs can take it in turns to guide their peers through what they have written, highlighting how the work meets the demands of the mark scheme as they do.

Bloom's Taxonomy

28 Bloom's Taxonomy of Educational Objectives underpins many of the mark schemes used at GCSE (and beyond). The taxonomy ranks different educational objectives from the simplest to the most complex (knowledge; comprehension; application; analysis; synthesis; evaluation – although many people feel the top two are interchangeable).

Take a look at a range of mark schemes when you have a chance and you will notice how the higher marks are awarded for analysis, synthesis and evaluation. Hence, it is worth focussing on these skills if we want to help students secure A and B grades. We will examine this in more detail in the next three entries.

For more on Bloom's Taxonomy have a look at my free resource, The Bloom-Buster.

Analysis

29 Analysis is a key part of achieving high marks in many GCSE papers. This means it is useful to regularly include analysis tasks as part of your teaching, so as to train students in how to use these skills. Here are a range of keywords you can use as the basis for analysis tasks, questions and activities:

Analyse; Categorize; Compare; Contrast; Differentiate; Discriminate; Distinguish; Examine; Experiment; Explore; Investigate; Question; Research; Scrutinize; Test.

Synthesis

30 As with analysis, so too with synthesis. Here are a range of keywords you can use as the basis for synthesis tasks, questions and activities:

Combine; Compose; Construct; Create; Devise; Design; Formulate; Hypothesise; Integrate; Merge; Organise; Plan; Propose; Synthesise; Unite.

Evaluation

31 And once again! As with synthesise and analysis, so too with evaluation. Here are a range of keywords you can use as the basis for evaluation tasks, questions and activities:

Appraise; Argue; Assess; Critique; Defend; Evaluate; Gauge; Grade; Inspect; Judge; Justify; Rank; Rate; Review; Value.

A and B Grade Checklists

32 You can create checklists detailing what is required from a piece of work if it is to receive an A or B grade and then share these with students in the form of hand-outs or wall displays. In either case, the purpose is to present pupils with a simple list they can use to help plan their work.

Here, you are doing the analysis of what is required on behalf of students and then communicating this to them in a simple form.

Problem-Solving Techniques

33 If we want our students to secure A and B grades then it is likely they will have to solve problems as part of the process. These problems might be specific questions in exams or they might be more general issues such as how to approach a piece of work.

Providing pupils with problem-solving techniques is a great way to help them bridge the gap between what they can do and what they need to do. You can develop problem-solving techniques for your own subject and then teach these to your students.

Common techniques include trial and error, testing of hypotheses, trying three different solutions, and breaking a problem down into smaller parts before dealing with each of these in turn.

SMART Targets

34 SMART targets are targets which are Specific; Measurable; Attainable; Relevant; and Time-Bound.

When you set targets for your pupils, or when they set targets for themselves designed to help them secure A and B grades, make sure they are SMART targets.

This will increase the likelihood that those targets will be met and that they will be effective.

Target Tracking

35 One of the risks with targets is that you or your students lose track of them. This can happen easily for example if you write targets in students' books, beneath a piece of work they have done. It may be that pupils simply forget the target is written there as they go on to produce more work.

As an alternative, provide each student with a sheet of paper containing a grid into which they can write the targets you set them as they go along. They can keep this at the front of their books, making it easier to track and refer to the targets you set.

Focus on Effort and Persistence

36 It is tempting to assume that A and B grades are a direct function of students producing great work. This is only half-true. The majority of A and B grades are actually a result of effort and persistence on the part of pupils, with the great work stemming from this.

In order to develop effort, persistence and grit in your classes, praise it whenever you see it. This will do two things. First, it will positively reinforce the behaviours you want to see from your students, meaning they will be more likely to be repeated. Second, it will habituate pupils into seeing effort, persistence and grit as important things they need to focus on.

Build Confidence

37 Confidence is all important when it comes to exams. If students enter exams feeling unconfident then they are less likely to perform to the standards of which they are capable.

But how can you build confidence? Here are five ideas to try out:

- As noted in the last entry, praise students' effort, grit and persistence.

- Do plenty of exam practice so that pupils know exactly what to expect in the exam.

- Rehearse what to do and how to respond if things go wrong.

- Encourage self-reflection and metacognition so that students feel in control of their learning.

- Make sure pupils know precisely what is expected of them and how they can achieve this.

Problem Forecasting

38 We are working under the assumption that, ultimately, all the work we do in lessons aimed at helping pupils to secure A and B grades will come to fruition when they sit their GCSE examinations.

With this in mind, it is well worth spending some time problem forecasting with your pupils.

This involves discussing all the potential problems which might arise in the examination hall, with regard to the various papers students need to sit in your subject, and identifying how best to deal with each one.

The technique is similar to that used by some athletes prior to competition. It helps to clear the mind of anxiety while also presenting a range of positive solutions to potential problems which might arise.

Hard Work

39 The harder you work, the better you will do. If you want to help students secure A and B grades at GCSE, make sure they work hard. Cultivate an atmosphere of hard work and dedication in your lessons; motivate pupils so that they feel they are putting the effort in for themselves rather than for an extrinsic goal (as this has been shown to have better long-term effects).

Make It Fun

40 And you can offset the hard work by making things fun.

To illustrate this point, consider the difference between a job which is remorselessly hard work and one requiring similar levels of effort but with a bit of laughter and humour mixed in.

When it comes to the former we feel fed up and tired but, in the latter, we don't mind so much. The fun factor takes our mind off things for a few minutes here and there, re-energising us and replenishing our motivation levels.

Self-Reporting

41 In John Hattie's research into the relative impact of different teaching interventions on student achievement, self-reporting of grades came out near the top. It was one of the most significant interventions in terms of the gains it led to.

Self-reporting involves asking pupils to assess themselves and identify honestly what grade or level they are working at. Invariably, students have an excellent understanding of where they are at.

Having asked pupils to self-report, you can then ask them to identify what they need to do to improve before setting up activities in which they can put these improvements into practice.

Repeating this self-report and improvement cycle should lead to continuous progression.

Get the Parents On-Board

42 This is sometimes one of the most difficult things to do. If you can manage it (or if it is the case already, which is great) then your students will have a ready-made support network to help them with revision, homework, exam preparation and so forth.

Three ways to help get parents on-board are:

- Talk to them at parent's evening about what they can do to help their child.

- Send home advice and tips on how to do well in your subject.

- Invite parents of GCSE students in to school to hear about what their children need to do to secure A and B grades in your subject.

Role Models

43 Here's a really simple yet effective technique to try.

Invite students who secured A and B grades the previous year to come and talk to your current pupils. Ask them to explain what they did which led to them achieving good grades and then facilitate a question and answer session.

Planned Revision

44 One of the risks with revision is that it can lack purpose. This is most clearly evident when students revise so as to be revising, rather than revise so as to reinforce and secure their understanding in preparation for the exams. As you will note, these are two subtly different things.

Take some time out in lessons to talk to students about how best to revise. Then, work with them to help them plan their revision. Highlight the benefits which stem from planning in advance what to revise, how to revise it, where to revise it and why to revise it.

Students Teach Others

45 One of the best ways to ensure you remember information is to teach it. We know this from our own experiences and we can call on this to assist pupils in their revision.

Explain the benefits of teaching ideas and information to other people and then encourage students to do it as part of their revision. They could teach their parents, siblings or friends in short ten or twenty minute bursts.

Alternatively, you might like to plan student teaching activities into the revision lessons you teach. This will serve to help pupils secure their knowledge and provide them with a model they can use to revise at home.

Subject Knowledge Audit

46 Give each pupil in your class a list of everything they have studied as part of the course. Ask them to go through and assign themselves a mark out of ten for how confident they feel with each section (1 = very unconfident; 10 = very confident).

Having finished the audit, students will have in their possession a document they can use to guide their revision. Clearly it will make sense to focus first on those topics which received the lowest marks before working up to the ones with higher marks and so on.

Practice, Practice, Practice

47 The more practice you get students to do, the better.

Use exam practice with them in lessons.

Encourage them to practice writing answers at home (or doing whatever is appropriate if the exam is practical).

Extol the virtues of practice over and again; this will help to cultivate the right mindset in your pupils.

A and B Grade Revision Guides

48 As a revision activity to do in class, ask students to work in pairs to create revision guides for the topics you have studied. Provide appropriate mark schemes and explain to pupils that these revision guides should be aimed solely at students seeking to secure A and B grades (i.e. themselves!).

As pupils are working on their guides, walk around the room and ask them to explain to you why each section is apt for A and B grades as opposed to being generic. This will cause students to reflect critically on what they are doing, further reinforcing the ideas in their minds.

Example Exam Scripts

49 This can be somewhat time-consuming but can bring significant rewards.

Take a past paper, sit yourself down and produce a model exam script.

You can then photocopy this, distribute it to the students in your class and talk them through it, explaining how and why it meets the criteria for an A grade.

Alternatively, you can distribute it to students along with a mark scheme and ask them to work in pairs to assess and annotate it. This process will help them internalise the demands of the mark scheme at the same time as it provides them with a series of relevant examples of how to succeed in each section.

Memorisation Techniques

50 And so we come to the conclusion of our whistle-stop tour through the avenues and alleyways of securing A and B grades at GCSE. Our final entry concerns an age-old method used to secure exam success: memorisation techniques. Here are five approaches you can share with your students:

- Mnemonic devices such as Richard Of York Gave Battle In Vain (Red, Orange, Yellow, Green, Blue, Indigo, Violet).

- Narrative (where one turns separate pieces of information into a story).

- Combining images and words (here, the dual demands on memory help create strong impressions).

- Active repetition such as writing, teaching or discussing.

- Mind-Maps (see entry 16).

All of these approaches can help pupils to better remember key information relevant to their examinations.

A Brief Request

If you have found this book useful I would be delighted if you could leave a review on Amazon to let others know.

If you have any thoughts or comments, or if you have an idea for a new book in the series you would like me to write, please don't hesitate to get in touch at mike@mikegershon.com.

Finally, don't forget that you can download all my teaching and learning resources for **FREE** at www.mikegershon.com.

Printed in Great Britain
by Amazon.co.uk, Ltd.,
Marston Gate.